Contents

Family ties

I come from a large family of animals called rodents. I am related to mice, hamsters and rats. Some people call me a guinea pig and some call me a cavy. I am just one of the many beautiful types of pet guinea pig.

All about me

Surprising speed
I may not look like a fast mover, but I can run very quickly if I want to. I stand up tall and scuttle along with surprising speed.

Shy but sweet
I tend to be quite nervous, and get a bit scared in open spaces. As long as you are calm and gentle with me and let me get used to you slowly, I will soon become braver.

Tough teeth

Like other rodents, my teeth never stop growing. I need to spend a lot of time chewing and gnawing to stop them getting too long. If my teeth do grow too long, I will not be able to eat properly and I may get ill.

Tail talk
Unlike most other animals, I do not have a tail. I don't climb as much as other rodents, so I don't need a tail for balance.

Hair not fur
My coat is quite rough, so it is known as hair, not fur.

What you see is what you get!

Super senses
I can smell and hear much better than you. My eyesight is very good, too. I notice any quick movements all around me – even above my head!

A little help
You will need an adult to help you take care of me. He or she will make sure that we are both safe and well, and that we do not hurt each other by mistake.

Coats and colours

It takes all sorts

All guinea pigs are the same basic shape and size, but our coats come in lots of different colours, lengths, patterns and styles. There are about 25 types, or breeds, of pet guinea pig.

American Crested
These guinea pigs have a short coat with a swirl of hair on top of their head.

Tricolour
My Tricolour friends have a coat of three different colours, one of which is always white.

Where's the hair?
The Skinny guinea pig has hair only on its face and paws. Hairless and Baldwin guinea pigs have almost no hair at all. They all feel the cold and need special care.

Kinds of coat

Guinea pigs can have short, long or even curly hair. Short-haired guinea pigs are easier to care for because they need less grooming.

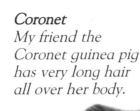

Coronet
My friend the Coronet guinea pig has very long hair all over her body.

Rex
These guinea pigs have a short, curly coat and curly whiskers.

I think I fancy a change of hair style.

Pet pair
Not every guinea pig is a special type. We are mixtures of more than one type. We are known as mixed-breeds, and we make beautiful pets.

8

Is it safe? I'm coming out to play!

My wild cousins

Wild guinea pigs live in Peru and Bolivia in South America. They live in groups and eat grass and other plants. Wild guinea pigs nest in small gaps between rocks or in burrows left behind by other animals.

Nature's way

Happy in hay
Like my wild cousins, I love to hide in long grass and hay. It makes me feel safe.

Bolt hole
Wild guinea pigs are hunted by other animals and need safe places to hide. I also need a place to go when I am scared. A nest box or a pile of hay is ideal.

LOOK OUT!
* **Never chase me** – I might get confused and think that you are hunting me. I will be scared and will try to dash for cover. I could hurt myself or get very stressed and unwell.

Part of the gang
My wild cousins depend on each other for warmth, company and safety – they warn each other if they sense danger.

Wild instincts
I am the same as a wild guinea pig in many ways. I like to spend lots of time nibbling plants and nesting, and I need the company of other guinea pigs. Like my wild cousins, I am most active at dawn and dusk.

All you need

Bottle and bowl
I will need a large drip-feed water bottle. If you put my water in a bowl, I will make a mess. I will also need a food bowl – something I cannot tip up or chew is best.

Basic requirements
Before you bring me home, you must get some basic supplies. I will need a hutch, a nest box and a run to play in. I will also need a litter tray, litter, food, a bowl, a water bottle, bedding and a friend to keep me company.

Ahh, time for another nap I think.

Best nest
My nest box should be cosy, but not too small. Make sure that the door is wide enough for me.

In or out?
If I live in the garden, my hutch needs to be weather-proof and sturdy enough to keep me safe from other animals. Place it in a shady, sheltered spot. If I live inside, keep my hutch away from sunlight and radiators.

Hot and cold
Whether I live inside or outside, it is important that I do not get too hot, too cold or damp. I need lots of dry bedding in the winter and plenty of shade in the summer.

Bedding down
Line the floor of my hutch with wood shavings, and my litter tray with paper- or wood-based litter. Hay is the best nesting material because I can eat it too.

Fresh hay

Wood-based litter

Wood shavings

Things to do
A hutch with different levels and places to explore will keep me busy.

Ideal home
Choose the largest hutch you have space for. One with large doors or a removable roof will be most practical.

Pick a piggy

Sows and boars

Male guinea pigs are called boars and female guinea pigs are called sows. Boars have two round openings under their tail. Sows have one round opening and one small narrow one.

Boar

Sow

Finding me

It is best to get your guinea pig from a good breeder or an animal shelter. They will give you tips about caring for your new pet. It is also a good idea to get information from books, websites and the vet.

Young ones

At six weeks old, baby guinea pigs are ready to leave their mother and go to a new home.

Playful piggies

Choose an active, playful guinea pig. If I seem very quiet and shy, it might mean that I am not well.

Pick a pair
I will be happiest if I live with another guinea pig of the same sex. If I am lonely I might get unwell.

Signs of good health
I am very healthy. My coat, eyes, ears, nose, mouth and bottom are clean. Pick a healthy guinea pig like me.

Who's that climbing over my tunnel?

LOOK OUT!
* **Never buy** a guinea pig with a runny nose or eyes, bald patches or diarrhoea.
* **Do not** choose a guinea pig that has been living in a damp, dirty or crowded hutch – he or she may be unwell.

Time for tea!

Feed me!

I love eating – it is my favourite way to pass the time! Fresh hay is the most important part of my diet. It keeps my tummy and teeth healthy. Make sure I always have a good supply of hay to nibble on.

Green, green grass
I need to eat fresh grass
every day if possible.
I will happily spend the
day munching away
in a run on the lawn.

LOOK OUT!
* **Never feed me** lawn cuttings – they can make my tummy fill up with gas and make me very ill.
* **Don't give me** rabbit food – it does not contain all the vitamins I need and can make me ill.

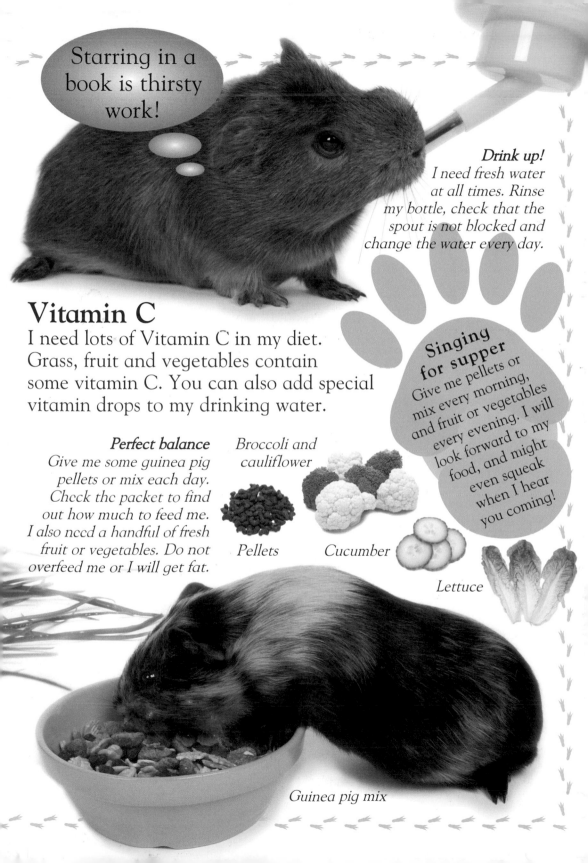

Starring in a book is thirsty work!

Drink up!
I need fresh water at all times. Rinse my bottle, check that the spout is not blocked and change the water every day.

Vitamin C
I need lots of Vitamin C in my diet. Grass, fruit and vegetables contain some vitamin C. You can also add special vitamin drops to my drinking water.

Singing for supper
Give me pellets or mix every morning, and fruit or vegetables every evening. I will look forward to my food, and might even squeak when I hear you coming!

Perfect balance
Give me some guinea pig pellets or mix each day. Check the packet to find out how much to feed me. I also need a handful of fresh fruit or vegetables. Do not overfeed me or I will get fat.

Broccoli and cauliflower

Pellets

Cucumber

Lettuce

Guinea pig mix

Clean out

A clean, dry hutch with plenty of fresh bedding will help to keep me happy and healthy. Damp bedding can make my paws sore and make it hard for me to breathe. Dirty bedding attracts flies and germs, and could make me ill.

Squeaky clean

Daily hay
Give me fresh hay every day. I will not eat damp or dirty hay.

Keep me safe

Make sure you put me somewhere safe while you clean out my hutch. I will be fine in a pet carrier for a short time, but if the weather is nice I will be happier outside in my run.

LOOK OUT!

* **Don't use** scented wood shavings in my hutch – they could give me breathing problems.
* **Clean my** hutch more often in the summer to help keep flies away.

A clean home is a happy home!

The routine

Remove any wet or dirty bedding and any uneaten food every day. Give my hutch a full clean-out at least once a week, more often if it starts to smell.

Sweep it out
Sweep or scoop out the dirty bedding and food from my hutch and throw it away.

Litter training

As long as my hutch is big enough, I will keep my bed, eating and toilet areas separate. If you put a litter tray in my toilet area, I will soon get used to using it.

Litter tray
Empty my litter tray every time you clean out my hutch – more often if it gets dirty.

Wipe it up
Wipe my hutch, litter tray and any toys with a damp cloth. Put in fresh bedding and litter when everything is dry.

Well groomed
If you see me grooming myself, it means I am feeling relaxed. I also groom my guinea pig friends to show them that I like them. If I try to groom you, it means I like you too!

I say!

Piggy signs

Guinea pigs talk to each other using a mixture of body language and sounds. If you spend enough time with me, you will soon learn to understand what I am trying to say.

Fighting talk
I usually get on well with other guinea pigs, but I might fight if I feel scared or threatened. If you hear me chattering my teeth or hissing, I am about to fight.

Shove off
If I want to be left alone, I will make a chattering or rumbling noise and try to hide from you. I will push up my head if you touch me. When I want you to pet me, I will stretch out in front of you and make quiet grunting sounds.

What's that smell? Is it food?

Curious creature
When I feel curious, I will hold my head up high and sniff the air. I might grunt, too. If I sense danger, I will chatter my teeth.

Having fun
When I am happy and having fun, I will run about with my guinea pig friends and touch noses with them. I might even jump, squeak and grunt!

LOOK OUT!
* **If I sit** with my body all hunched up and do not want to play, I may be ill.
* **Listen carefully** to the sounds I make. If I squeak very loudly it may mean that I am in pain.

Scared signs
If I am a bit scared, I will try to hide. If I am very scared, I will keep very still. My body will go stiff and I will make loud squeaking noises.

Getting to know you

I can be quite shy at first, but as I
get used to you I will become more
relaxed around you. Be patient
and let me make friends in
my own time. It will
be well worth
the wait!

Gently does it
Pick me up gently by sliding
one hand right under my body
and holding me steady with
the other. Hold me close to
your body when you
carry me around.

Hold me close

Tempting treats

Giving me treats is a good way to win my trust. Hold out the treat in your hand and wait for me to come and get it. You will soon find that I come running every time I hear you opening the packet!

Gentle nature

I am very gentle and it is unusual for me to bite or scratch. If I try to bite you when you pick me up or touch me, it probably means I am either very scared or in pain.

> I'll do anything for a bit of banana!

Guinea pig treats

Dried fruit mix

Healthy nibbles
Give me only small amounts of healthy treats, or I will get fat.

LOOK OUT!
* **Always hold** me carefully with both hands. If I struggle or fall, I could hurt myself.
* **Never squeeze** me around my tummy – you could seriously hurt me.

Keeping me busy

As long as I live in a large hutch with at least one other guinea pig I will not get bored. Give me lots of attention and interesting things to nibble. If you let me out to play as often as possible I will be a very happy guinea pig!

Lots to do

From the shops
I love toys that I can chew on and toys that you can stuff with grass or hay. They keep me busy and are good for my teeth.

Home made
I don't need expensive toys. An empty toilet roll stuffed with hay will keep me happy for hours!

Talk to me
I am very friendly and talkative. Try to stop and say hello every time you pass my hutch. I will be pleased to see you and might even squeak 'hello' back to you!

Do you want to come for a scamper?

No thanks, I'm busy munching.

Room to roam

I will enjoy getting some exercise and fresh air in a safe run in the garden or exploring a safe area in your house. I need a shelter to hide in wherever I am.

LOOK OUT!
* **Make sure** that my run is safe from cats and dogs.
* **If you** let me run free in the house, put any electric wires or poisonous plants out of my reach so that I cannot chew them.

Fit and well

Paw check
Check my paws to make sure my claws are not too long and my pads are not sore.

Getting to know me
If you spend lots of time with me, you will be able to tell if I am not feeling well. If my behaviour changes and you are worried about me, speak to the vet.

Perfect coat
Groom me every day. Check my coat and skin for sore or bald patches.

Health routine

The best way to keep me healthy is to watch me very carefully. Check me over every day when you pick me up. If you notice something unusual or feel at all worried about me, take me to the vet.

Bottom check
Check my bottom every day. It should be clean and dry. If it looks sore or dirty, take me to see the vet.

Clear ears
My ears should be nice and clean. If you see me scratching them a lot I might have mites. Do not put anything down my ears unless the vet tells you to.

Eyes and nose
Check that my eyes are not runny, cloudy or closed. Check that my nose is not runny. If you see me sneezing a lot take me to the vet.

It's really tasty, you should try it!

Tough teeth
My teeth never stop growing, so I need to chew things to stop them getting too long. Check my mouth to make sure my gums are not sore and my teeth are not getting very long.

LOOK OUT!
* **If I stop** eating or start to dribble, it may mean that my teeth are too long.
* **I need** to see the vet straight away if I am very quiet, have an upset tummy or stop eating and drinking.

Other pets

I am a friendly animal and will get on well with most other pets. They may not always get on with me though, so introduce us carefully. Never trust a cat or dog with me – it might think I look like dinner!

Bunny buddy
I like rabbits, but it is not a good idea to leave us alone together. Rabbits tend to be rough when they play, and can kick hard.

Two's company

LOOK OUT!

* **Guinea pigs** sometimes bully each other. If you see my hutch mates pulling out my hair or fighting with me, ask the vet for some advice. I might become unhappy or ill if I am being bullied.

A friend in need
If you look after me well and treat me gently, we will become very good friends.

Never alone

Like my wild cousins, I need lots of company. I will feel lonely and unhappy if I have to spend too much time by myself. If I am unhappy, I am more likely to become unwell.

Best mates

Other guinea pigs make the best friends for me. We can live together and keep each other company when you are not around. It is best to keep me with other guinea pigs of the same sex. If you have a mixture of boars and sows, you will end up with lots of babies!

Peaceful meetings
The best way to introduce me to other guinea pigs is just to put us in our hutch together. Make sure that we each have a place to hide if we need to.

Are you sure there's room for two in here?

Yes, just breathe in and snuggle up!

Babies on board
Pregnant guinea pigs get very big when they are close to giving birth. They need extra food and find it hard to move around. They must be handled with care.

Little piggies

Having babies

Sows can get pregnant at three weeks of age and should always have their first babies before they are eight months old. Guinea pigs usually have three or four babies, but they can have just one or as many as eight!

Think carefully
Only let your guinea pigs have babies if you know you can find them all good homes. If you do not want your guinea pigs to have babies, the vet can give them an operation.

Newborn baby
Baby guinea pigs are born with hair, claws and teeth. Their eyes are open and they can move around straight away. Their mother provides them with milk and warmth.

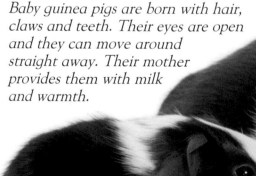

Phew! Thank goodness I only had one baby!

Growing up

Baby guinea pigs start to nibble adult food soon after they are born. By the time they are three weeks old, they do not need their mother's milk at all. At three weeks, the boars and sows should be split up to stop them from having babies.

Leaving home

Guinea pigs are ready to leave their mother and go to a new home when they are about six weeks old.

Glossary

bedding
This is the soft material that is used to make a guinea pig's hutch warm and comfortable.

boar
A boar is a male guinea pig.

body language
Guinea pigs use their bodies to show other guinea pigs and people what they are thinking and feeling. This is called body language.

coat
An animal's hair or fur is known as its coat. Guinea pigs' coats can come in different colours, patterns and lengths.

grooming
When you brush a guinea pig's coat it is called grooming. Guinea pigs also groom themselves and each other to keep clean.

handling
When you pick up your guinea pig it is called handling. There is a special way to handle guinea pigs so that you do not hurt them.

hay
Hay is dried grass. It is full of goodness and keeps longer than fresh grass.

nest
A nest is the place where guinea pigs hide, sleep and have babies.

pregnant
When a female guinea pig is pregnant, it means she has babies growing inside her.

rodent
Guinea pigs belong to a family of animals called rodents. Hamsters, mice and rats are also rodents.

sow
A sow is a female guinea pig.

veterinary surgeon
A veterinary surgeon, or vet, is an animal doctor. You should take your guinea pig to the vet if you are worried that it might be ill or injured.

vitamin
A substance found in food that helps animals stay healthy.

Find out more ...

Websites

www.bluecross.org.uk
Animal welfare charity
website with information
on animal adoption,
volunteering and events,
as well as a fun kids' page.

www.allaboutpets.org.uk
Website for The Blue Cross's
pet-care information service,
giving pet owners access to
more than 70 downloadable
pet-care leaflets.

www.comfycavies.com
A guinea pig
website full
of information
on housing,
healthcare,
grooming,
feeding and
much more.
It even has a chat
room for members,
an online shop and
a gallery where you can
post your piggy's picture.

Addresses

The Blue Cross
Head Office
Shilton Road
Burford
Oxon
OX18 4PF

PDSA
Whitechapel Way
Priorslee
Telford
Shropshire
TF2 9PQ

I know it all
already, I'm off to
find my dinner!

Index

Honeysuckle Cottage
Poppy's House

Forget-Me-Not Cottage
Grandpa's House and Office

Poppy Field

Honeypot Cottage
Honey and Granny Bumble's House

Blossom
Bakehouse

Cornsilk Castle
and Courtyard

Village Hall

Sage's
Vet Surgery

Post Office

River Swan

Beehive
Beauty Salon

Burley Farm
The Meadowsweets' House

Riverside
Stables

Honeypot Hill
Railway Station

To Camomile Cove
via Periwinkle Lane

N
W   E
S

Join Princess Poppy on more adventures . . .

★ Ballet Shoes ★

★ Twinkletoes ★

★ The Fair Day Ball ★

THE BIRTHDAY
A PICTURE CORGI BOOK: 978 0 552 55335 3 (from January 2007)
0 552 55335 2

First published in Great Britain by Picture Corgi,
an imprint of Random House Children's Books

This edition published 2006

3 5 7 9 10 8 6 4 2

Text copyright © Janey Louise Jones, 2006
Illustration copyright © Picture Corgi Books, 2006
Illustrations by Veronica Vasylenko
Design by Tracey Cunnell

The right of Janey Louise Jones to be identified as the author of this work has been
asserted in accordance with the Copyright, Designs and Patents Act 1988.

Picture Corgi Books are published by Random House Children's Books,
61–63 Uxbridge Road, London W5 5SA,
a division of The Random House Group Ltd, in Australia by Random House Australia (Pty) Ltd,
20 Alfred Street, Milsons Point, Sydney, NSW 2061, Australia,
in New Zealand by Random House New Zealand Ltd,
18 Poland Road, Glenfield, Auckland 10, New Zealand,
and in South Africa by Random House (Pty) Ltd,
Isle of Houghton, Corner Boundary Road & Carse O'Gowrie, Houghton 2198, South Africa
THE RANDOM HOUSE GROUP Limited Reg. No. 954009
www.kidsatrandomhouse.co.uk
www.princesspoppy.com

A CIP catalogue record for this book is available from the British Library.

Printed in China

The Birthday

Written by Janey Louise Jones

PICTURE CORGI

For Emma Brown,
who was a true princess

The Birthday

featuring

Honey
★

Grandpa
★

Mum
★

Princess Poppy

Granny Bumble
★

Dad
★

Saffron Thimble
★

Poppy woke up early.

"YIPPEE! It's my birthday!" she shouted as she jumped out of bed.

"I love birthdays," said Poppy. "Today I can be a special princess all day long!"

Poppy looked around her room — toys, books and dressing-up clothes were scattered all over the place, but she couldn't see any sign of a present.

Hmmmm, nothing for a birthday princess in here.

"I do hope everyone has remembered my birthday," she sighed.

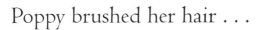

Poppy brushed her hair . . .

put on her favourite red dress . . .

and put her poppy hairclips on.

"I'm off to find my birthday things!" she announced,
and rushed off to her parents' room.

"Mum, Dad, I'm here," said Poppy.

"Oh, Poppy, I'm still sleepy," said a muffled voice from under the bedcovers.

"But it's my birth—" Poppy began.

"Go back to bed for half an hour," mumbled Mum.

"It *is* only seven o'clock in the morning, Poppy," groaned Dad.

"How could Mum and Dad sleep late on my special day?" wondered Poppy, crossly.

She went back to lie on her bed. "This is so boring," grumped the birthday girl.

So she decided to go next door and see Granny Bumble — she was always up early.

When Poppy arrived, there were lots of freshly chopped strawberries on the table and Granny Bumble was beating sugar and butter in a big bowl.

"Hello, Granny Bumble, it's my birth—"

"Poppy, can't you see I'm in the middle of something?

Run along now, I'll see you later," she smiled.

Even Granny Bumble doesn't care that it's my birthday.

"Right, that's it!" Poppy decided. "I'm going to see Grandpa.
At least *he* would never forget my birthday."

Poppy walked through the big door into Grandpa's office
and found him hiding behind a huge newspaper.

"Can't talk, dear!" said Grandpa. "I'm stuck on my crossword!"

Poppy marched out and closed the door with a BANG!
Not Grandpa too.

"And his newspaper was upside down!" she said.

Next, Poppy peeped into the window of the sewing shop. Her cousin Saffron was busy stitching a beautiful red ball dress.

"Hi, Saffron, that looks gorgeous! Did you know it's—"

"Poppy, I'm sorry, but I've really got to get on with this job,"
said Saffron. "This is for a girl who can't wait for anything.
I don't have time to chat."

Even Saffron is too busy!

So Poppy went to the Lavender Garden to find her best friend Honey . . .

Honey was dressed up in her fairy outfit.

"Please tell me *you* have remembered my birthday," pleaded Poppy.

"Oh, Poppy, I haven't forgotten, but I haven't exactly remembered, if you see what I mean," said Honey, sounding a bit confused.

Poor Poppy felt so sad. It was as if no one cared enough about her to remember her special day.

"I just don't understand it," she said. "Mum *always* says I'm a special princess on my birthday."

Suddenly Honey jumped up. "Come with me, Poppy. Let's go and play in the courtyard."

As they got closer to the courtyard, they heard beautiful music playing.

Honey opened the gates . . .

Streamers, balloons and flower petals showered down on Poppy's head.

"Bang!" went the party poppers.

"Happy Birthday!" shouted Poppy's family and friends.

"WOW!" laughed Poppy.
"Thank you! You *have* remembered!"

"You've waited very patiently, darling," said Mum.

"Now you can open all your lovely presents!"

Mum gave Poppy a bright red velvet box.

Inside was a glittering necklace.

Poppy put it on.

"It's so sparkly! Thanks, Mum! Thanks, Dad!"

Granny Bumble stepped forward with a birthday sponge cake decorated with fresh strawberries and cream.

Poppy blew out the glowing candles, then she tasted a slice.

"Mmm, deeeelicious!"

Grandpa handed Poppy a gorgeous tiara with three poppies on it. Poppy put it on.

"I love it! Thanks, Grandpa!"

Then Saffron gave Poppy a huge white box, covered in poppies, with a red bow on top.

Poppy opened the box, and pulled out a red princess ball dress and red velvet shoes.

"Oh, Saffron, it *was* for me! Thank you!" exclaimed Poppy.

"I thought you said it was for a girl who can't wait for anything!"

Everyone started to laugh.

"But Poppy," said Honey, "it's only just after breakfast time now and you *have* been finding it hard to wait for your presents, haven't you?"

"Maybe a little bit," giggled Poppy. "I should have known something lovely was going to happen."

Honey then handed her friend a small glass bottle with a red ribbon tied around it.

"It's petal perfume," Honey explained. "I made it myself."

"Oh, Honey, it smells lovely!" Poppy said as she dabbed the perfume behind her ears.

Then Poppy dashed off to try on her princess dress and red velvet shoes.

"Poppy, you are the most beautiful princess ever," said Grandpa as she showed off all her wonderful presents.

"Grandpa," Poppy asked, "is *every* little girl a princess?"

"Yes, Poppy, every girl is a princess, especially on her birthday!"

Poppy did a little twirl. "What a perfect Princess Poppy Party!"

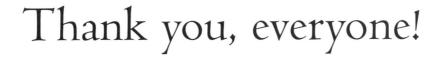

Thank you, everyone!